impressionist

mary cassatt

at home

Barbara Stern Shapiro

UNIVERSE

Front cover:
Tea, 1879–1880
Back cover:
Lydia at a Tapestry Frame, c. 1881
Page 1:
Woman Reading (detail), 1878–1879
Facing page:
Breakfast in Bed (detail), 1897
Pages 6–7:
The Garden (detail), 1880–1881
Page 8:
Portrait of a Lady (detail), 1878
Pages 12–13:
Portrait of a Little Girl (detail), 1878
Page 80:
Nude Child (detail), 1890–1891

First published in the United States of America in 1998 by
UNIVERSE PUBLISHING
A Division of Rizzoli International Publications, Inc.
300 Park Avenue South
New York, NY 10010

98 99 00 / 10 9 8 7 6 5 4 3 2 1

Library of Congress Catalog Card Number: 98-60982

Design by Nicky Lindeman for Mirko Ilić Corp.

Printed in Singapore

NOTE TO THE READER

Mary Cassatt: Impressionist at Home *is published on the occasion of the exhibition* Mary Cassatt: Modern Woman, *organized by The Art Institute of Chicago, the Museum of Fine Arts, Boston, and the National Gallery of Art, Washington D. C. The titles for the works of art cited in this book are based upon the research and checklist prepared by my colleagues at The Art Institute of Chicago. They have generally assigned titles that were used in the first public exhibition of a given work. In a few instances, I have included a more familiar title when one was employed during the lifetime of the artist. Reference to the 1998 exhibition catalog for scholarly, in-depth information is strongly recommended.*

Every acknowledgment must be made to Nancy Mowll Mathews, whose writings on the life of Mary Cassatt are extensive. These works comprise articles, biographies, bibliographies, and collections of letters; in particular, I have used Cassatt: A Retrospective *(1996) and* Cassatt and Her Circle: Selected Letters *(1984). I am grateful to Malcolm A. Rogers and Patricia B. Jacoby, who encouraged me to undertake this project, as well as to my ever-patient and supportive husband. A special debt of thanks is due to a very helpful member of the Cassatt family, who wishes to remain anonymous.*

Barbara Stern Shapiro

contents

And it is a mark inherently special to her talent: Mlle. Cassatt, who is American, I believe, paints for us the French; but in her habitats so Parisian, she puts the welcoming smile of the "at home"; she gives to us in Paris what none of our painters would be able to express—the joyous quietude, the tranquil goodwill of an interior.

J.-K. Huysmans, in *L'Art moderne*, 1883[1]

It is accepted that Monet, Renoir, and Pissarro studied the cityscape, seascape, and landscape to capture the essence of Impressionism, the new art movement of which they were leading advocates. Mary Cassatt, in her personal exploration of this style, pursued the same aesthetic but used her home surroundings or interior scenes of fashionable life to create another aspect of Impressionism. Although she is primarily remembered for her numerous studies of mothers and children, the majority of Mary Cassatt's works are portraits of family members, close friends, or neighbors used as models for figure studies. She rarely accepted a portrait commission and seems to have been most productive and comfortable in her home or studio settings surrounded by members of her family and her possessions. Many of the objects depicted in Cassatt's paintings, pastels, and prints were treasured by her descendants and still exist. Of further interest are the backdrops, silver objects, ceramics, and furniture pieces that repeatedly appear in her works; all are from her Paris apartment or her country home in northern France. Given her close family relationships, it is understandable that her source of inspiration was nearby. She relied upon these intimate subjects—both human and inanimate—for her representations and regularly exhibited with her French colleagues who supported and approved of her personal artistic style and her "modern" techniques.

EMBRACING THE
IMPRESS

Mary Stevenson Cassatt was born May 22, 1844, to a fairly prominent family in Pittsburgh with strong ties to Philadelphia. Her family was well-off and led a way of life that became the scaffolding for most of her subject matter. She was part of a group of young artist-students who, seemingly unaffected by the Civil War, sailed for Europe, as did Cassatt in 1866, where they congregated in Paris. When the Franco-Prussian War erupted in 1870, they scattered to other countries or, like Cassatt, returned home to America to avoid the conflict. Late in 1871, Mary Cassatt set sail again, this time to Italy, to study the Old Master paintings in the museums there. She eventually traveled to Belgium, Spain, and the Netherlands, and settled in Paris after 1874. A mark of professional achievement for women artists was to study privately with a French professor, as did Cassatt with Jean-Léon Gérôme, and ultimately to have a major work accepted at the prestigious Paris Salon, a requisite that the young artist fulfilled in 1868, 1870, 1872, and then annually through 1876.

Had Cassatt adhered to a traditional mode, these accomplishments would already have established her as an artist of some repute, but her awareness of the radical "Impressionists" encouraged her to change direction. One of Cassatt's paintings at the 1874 Salon had attracted the attention of Edgar Degas, and when the Salon jury did not accept her work for 1877, she accepted her colleague's invitation to join the Impressionists. Thus began a forty-year association with an admired fellow artist as well as friendships with many of the most notable painters of the last quarter of the nineteenth century. What began as a journey of an American artist in Europe, refining her skills in order to return to American art circles, became a long-term sojourn as an Impressionist artist and a permanent expatriate. When Cassatt's immediate family moved to Paris at the end of 1877, a strong tie to France was established, and her embrace of a French lifestyle was complete.

Cassatt's debut with her new professional colleagues took place in 1879 in time for the fourth Impressionist exhibition; efforts to be ready for an exhibition in 1878 had been futile. Her preparations and submissions for the group show provide a critical understanding of the artist as an American, a member of the upper class in French society, and a woman who, along with her painter friend Berthe Morisot, had entered a masculine world. Her new painting style was so different from that of her earlier work that it is striking to witness the transformation. Her subject matter changed dramatically, her brushstrokes became patterns of colors and forms, and, most important, her palette was radically altered: the darkly painted subjects in Italian and Spanish costumes were abandoned forever.

A telling example of Cassatt's new style, painted in 1878 and submitted to the 1879 exhibition, is *Portrait of a Little Girl* (fig. 1). The style in which she presented the restless child, sprawling in a blue, upholstered chair, is in marked contrast to Cassatt's earlier formal paintings. The off-center view, uptilted floor, sparkling light, and fresh colors propelled Cassatt into a modern idiom. Degas's influence is not only recognizable in the asymmetrical composition but was confirmed by Cassatt herself when she later wrote that "he had worked on it." This painting of multiple blue flower–patterned chairs scattered throughout an otherwise sparsely furnished room is an example of Cassatt's affection for comfortable subjects "at home." The small dog asleep in the chair at left, offsetting the slightly bored child, is a Belgian griffon, a breed of dog favored by the artist throughout her life.

Of the eleven works exhibited by Mary Cassatt in the fourth Impressionist exhibition, five show young women in a theater setting. Her attraction to interior

Fig. 1: Portrait of a Little Girl, *1878*

Fig. 2: Woman in a Loge, *1878–1879*

Fig. 3: At the Français (a Sketch), *1877–1878*

scenes that reflected her fashionable life is similarly noted in the dramatic, enclosed environments where young debutantes discreetly hold fans. *Woman in a Loge*, 1878–1879 (fig. 2), captures the effect of a sumptuous hall glowing with light; the lush colors give the young model (possibly her sister Lydia), seated before a mirror, a prominence and beauty that one would not have expected in this public scene. In many respects, the lighting and elegance of Cassatt's Parisian apartment is repeated in the theater setting. One critic, Diego Martelli, commented favorably:

Fig. 4: Woman Reading, *1878–1879*

Cassatt is a young American who . . . seeks movement, light, and design in the most modern sense. Her half-figure of a woman in a theater box lit by gaslight and reflections from a mirror is a very beautiful work. [2]

Unlike Degas, who usually depicted the stage and its performers, Cassatt focused on the audience, with a special emphasis on a single figure. The painting *At the Français (a Sketch)*, 1877–1878 (fig. 3), exhibited in Boston in the same year that it was completed, reveals Cassatt's assured handling of the medium and an elegance of style. The woman in black at the opera observes a distant scene while summary dashes of paint indicate a man in another box who scrutinizes the model.

The portrait *Woman Reading*, 1878–1879 (fig. 4), evoked a number of laudatory comments at the "Independents" exhibition. (The same tufted armchair, here painted in bright green, appears in blue with the sprawling child in the earlier painting.) Although it was noted that Cassatt was a student of Degas, there was great interest in and commentary on her portraits for their own sake. Edmond Duranty claimed that "a most remarkable sense of elegance and distinction—and very English (she is American)—marks these portraits." [3] And further, Arsène Houssaye wrote: "*Woman Reading*, seen in profile, is a miracle of simplicity and elegance. There is nothing more graciously honest and aristocratic than her portraits of young women . . . ." [4]

Fig. 5: Edgar Degas, Mary Cassatt at the Louvre: The Etruscan Gallery, *1879–1880.*

A PRINTMAKING EXPERIENCE

For Cassatt, the outcome of the fourth exhibition was acceptance by her peers, some extra income, and a fervent desire to make prints for the next Impressionist exhibition, which would take place in the spring of 1880. Degas was the catalyst who convinced the artists working in his studio, including Cassatt, Camille Pissarro, and Félix Bracquemond, to prepare some etchings for the fifth exhibition. Cassatt abandoned her earlier, tentative etching style and mastered the complex procedures Degas had demonstrated. Her prolific production at this time attests to the skills of her teacher and her innate talent as a printmaker. Preliminary stages in the development of the print, called *états*, were appreciated and cherished, and in the spring of 1880 both Cassatt and Pissarro exhibited their working *états*. Cassatt's contribution to *Le Jour et la nuit*, the journal that Degas was promoting, was *Woman at the Theater*, 1879–1880 (fig. 6), based on a combination of her theater compositions. Two states of this print were shown in 1880,

Fig. 6: Woman at the Theater, *1879–1880*

Fig 7: Interior Scene, *c. 1879–1880*

along with other works that continued to illuminate Cassatt's preference for family scenes. Most of the etchings were intimate views of the life of a cultivated American who enjoyed gracious living. Her largest print, *Interior Scene*, about 1879–1880 (fig. 7), is an impressionist study in black and white. The shaded standing figure of a visitor is dynamically silhouetted against the lightly curtained window, while the seated hostess, drawn in darkness, anchors the social event. The combination of lines, hatchings, and grains on a single plate is daunting. It is this print that appears to merge the two "Mary Cassatt" prints that Degas had prepared for *Le Jour et la nuit*: *Mary Cassatt at the Louvre: The Etruscan Gallery* (fig. 5), and *Mary Cassatt at the Louvre: The Paintings Gallery* (fig. 9). In all three prints—the two by Degas and the one by Cassatt—there are fashionable, paired figures in social pursuits who are placed decisively in interior environments; Cassatt, however, depended on a more familiar domestic setting.

Bracquemond probably designed the cover for the portfolio of prints envisioned by the group, but no etching is clearly identified as his contribution. Nevertheless, he submitted some etchings to the 1880 exhibition that were decorative designs for a porcelain and faience service, probably the set produced by Haviland & Co. Cassatt owned a selection of these "Bracquemond" plates (fig. 8), some of which still belong to members of her family.

Fig. 8: Bracquemond tureen and plate

Fig. 9: Edgar Degas, Mary Cassatt at the Louvre:
The Paintings Gallery, *1879–1880*

PAINTING her WORLD

Even the three canvases exhibited in 1880 reveal Cassatt's preference for her "at-home" subjects. *Portrait of Madame J.* (fig. 11) was painted in 1879–1880; the black costume and the broad handling of the paint acknowledge the style of her friend and colleague, Edouard Manet. In his review of the fifth exhibition, Armand Silvestre noted that "[Mary Cassatt's] Portrait of Mme J . . . in a black dress, sitting on flowered cushions is a piquant little piece."[5] It is a handsome rendition of a model seated in one of Cassatt's familiar and beloved armchairs, upholstered with the recognizable flowered material. The stunning woman is a visitor to the Cassatt home, where she is posed before a framed, mounted fan (fig. 10)—almost certainly by Degas—that had been shown the previous year at the fourth Impressionist exhibition. Cassatt acquired the painting of the fan from Degas and kept it for many years before putting it on deposit with her longtime dealer, Durand-Ruel, in 1913. Eventually, it was sold with other Degas works to her close friend and great collector Louisine Havemeyer in 1918. A photograph of Mary Cassatt taken at her country house in Beaufresne by Theodate Pope in 1903 (fig. 13) depicts a setting similar to that of *Portrait of Madame J*, with the artist seated in front of her prized possession.

One is tempted to propose that Cassatt was aware of Manet's portrait, *Repose: Portrait of Berthe Morisot* (fig. 12). Although executed much earlier, in 1870, Cassatt could have seen the painting when it was exhibited at the Salon of 1873 and when it was in the collection of a friend, Théodore Duret, the well-known journalist and critic. Morisot, in her flowing white, floral-print dress, may well have served as a model for Cassatt's elegant young woman in black.

Mention should be made of a painting by Gustave Caillebotte entitled *Portrait of Mme H.* (location unknown), painted in 1877 and shown in the 1879 group exhibition. This work evokes class and social position; it depicts a well-dressed model in a respectable interior space who is, like Cassatt's Madame J., positioned in a three-quarter pose close to the viewer. Cassatt obviously knew this painting but chose the more dazzling portrait by Manet as the source for her image.

Another painting displayed in the fifth Impressionist exhibition, *Tea*, 1879–1880 (fig. 15) and then exhibited in 1893 at Galerie Durand-Ruel as *Five O'Clock*, is a fine demonstration of Mary Cassatt's mature style and clearly reflects the harmonious and gracious living of her bourgeois world. In an elegant drawing room, undoubtedly Cassatt's, the handsome silver tea service (fig. 14) acts as a foil and balance for the two fashionable young women who gaze contemplatively across

Fig. 10: Edgar Degas, Fan Mount: Ballet Girls, *1879*

Fig. 11: Portrait of Mme. J., *1879–1880*

the room. The model for the figure at left was the artist's sister Lydia, joined by a friend for a cup of tea at home. The off-center format and the differences in treatment between the sharply focused tea set and the more loosely rendered background reflect Degas's avant-garde principles, yet the juxtaposition of patterns, the attractive interior decoration (including a flowered-chintz sofa), and the more freely applied brushwork all demonstrate Mary Cassatt's unique interpretation of the Impressionist aesthetic. The silver service, made in Philadelphia, consists of six pieces (not all shown in the painting); three of these were initialed "M. S. 1813" and were probably given to her grandmother, Mary Stevenson. The remaining pieces may have been added upon the marriage of the artist's mother. Cassatt also featured this set in a preparatory drawing and, in reverse, in a print called *Lydia at Afternoon Tea* (fig. 16).

In reviews of the exhibition, several critics felt that the painting was an "excellent canvas"; Paul Mantz, however, was very harsh and complained that in order to add some realism, "Cassatt...placed a tray filled with necessary paraphernalia on a table.... It is poorly drawn, the tea service is misshapen. She did not know how to realize her idea. The wretched sugar bowl remains floating in the air like a dream."[6]

Regardless of this critical statement about *Tea*, this painting is, above all, a glimpse into the home of Cassatt and her family. It is a statement about the life of the artist surrounded by and responsible for the well-being and pleasure of members of her family. Although Louisine Havemeyer worried that Cassatt would be identified only by her privileged background and social teas, this extraordinary and serious painting is a window into her great talent, as well as her status and proper lifestyle.

Fig. 12: Edouard Manet, Repose: Portrait of Berthe Morisot, *c. 1870*

The silver service stands out with great clarity from the broadly painted fireplace mantel, ginger jar, and ornate picture/mirror frame. The striped wallpaper and fine white china suggest further elegant touches that are enhanced by the juxtaposition of the patterned interior against the simple and somber clothes of the women. Cassatt brought together a masterful picture through the use of loose but carefully layered brushstrokes and touches of color. Unlike Degas, who stood apart from his subjects, Cassatt has, in a serious manner, brought the viewer into her home. Another painting, also entitled *Tea*, 1879 (fig. 17), again depicts Lydia in this afternoon ritual, a study of exquisite Parisian fashion, gracefully holding a fine cup and saucer in her gloved hands. Exhibited in 1881 at the sixth impressionist exhibition, *Tea*, along with the artist's other entries, received strong praise, including Huysmans's comment: "add to this tender, private note a further delicate undertone of Parisian refinements."[7]

Five years earlier in November, 1876, May Alcott, sister of Louisa May Alcott, described a party at Cassatt's studio and her unchanging, respectable life. The guests partook of:

> ...fluffy cream and chocolate, with French cakes, while sitting in carved chairs, on Turkish rugs, with superb tapestries as a background, and fine pictures on the walls looking down from their splendid frames. Statues and articles of vertu filled the corners, the whole being lighted by a great antique hanging lamp. We sipped our *chocolat* from superior china, served . . . upon an embroidered cloth of heavy material. Miss Cassatt was charming as usual in two shades of brown satin and rep . . . .[8]

The urban figure, the decorative elements, and the intimate elegance continued to be integral elements in Cassatt's artistic endeavors.

It is worth noting that even when the painter recorded an outdoor scene such as *The Garden*, 1880 (fig. 18), the space is enclosed and delineated as if the subject was seated in a luxurious room. Lydia, who is crocheting in their garden at Marly, holds her needles instead of a small teacup, but the posture, attitude, elegant dress, and, most important, the brilliant brushstrokes and coloration are apparent in both paintings. Later, in 1893, the critic Gustave Geffroy would comment that Cassatt had a "refined way of seeing women and children in the light of gardens, in light-filled rooms veiled by blinds."[9]

Fig. 14: Silver tea service

Fig. 15: Tea, *1879–1880*

Fig. 16: Lydia at Afternoon Tea, *c. 1880*

Fig. 17: Tea, *1879*

INSPIRATION *close at home*

In 1881, Cassatt completed what was probably the final portrait of her sister before her death in November 1882. *Lydia Seated at a Tapestry Frame* (fig. 19) is another domestic view of this serious model who was devoted to her sister's artistic success.

Throughout her career, Cassatt's favorite subjects for portraits were members of her family. They functioned not only as representatives of an upper-class life but were superb models for modern paintings in the Impressionist manner. In 1878, Cassatt prepared a new portrait of her mother reading the Parisian daily newspaper, *Le Figaro*. The painting, *Portrait of a Lady* (fig. 20), presents many of Cassatt's typical compositional devices from the late 1870s and early 1880s: the flowered armchair, repeated in a number of family portraits; a framed object such as the mirror that reflects aspects of everyday life; and bravura brushwork, especially evident in the white dress with its shades of violet, cream, and gray.

One of Cassatt's most powerful and controversial portraits was *The Lady at the Tea Table*, 1883 (fig. 23), an excellent example of many of the aesthetic and life principles the artist embraced. Mary Dickinson Riddle, her mother's cousin from Pittsburgh, was asked by Cassatt to pose when she and her daughter visited Paris. Both women gave generous gifts to the Cassatt family, including one blue and white tea set from China (fig. 21), which became the focus of this major portrait. Mrs. Riddle, a formidable woman, was known for her handsome appearance and proper dress. Here the dark shape of her gown, reminiscent of Manet's palette, sets off the brilliant blue of her eyes, which, in turn, are accentuated by the strong color of the tea set. There is no question that the sitter is able to manage with finesse the many delicate pieces of china before her. Implications of stability

Fig. 18: The Garden, *1880*

Fig. 19: Lydia Seated at a Tapestry Frame, *1880–1881.*

Fig. 20: Portrait of a Lady, *1878*

and monumentality are established by the framed painting and molding that fill the background space. Cassatt combined a scene from "modern life" with her impressionist techniques: loose brushstrokes, touches of various colors that alter and enrich the white walls and tablecloth, and the ritualistic tea arrangement. Although Cassatt received many compliments on the painting, including praise from the difficult-to-please Degas, the Riddle family did not believe that the portrait did justice to their mother, who was a noted beauty; comments were made about Mrs. Riddle's "clawlike hands" (fig. 22). The number of times the tea set appears in Cassatt's work furthers our understanding of her attachment to "home" appurtenances; see, for example, *The Tea* (fig. 25), a drypoint made in 1889–1890, and the remarkable color print, *The Visit* (fig. 26), 1890–1891, where the tea set, laid out for an afternoon tea party, occupies pride of place. In the edition of the color print, the artist consistently applied touches of gold paint by hand to the rims on the cups and saucers, mimicking the refinement of the china set. It

Fig. 21 (top): China tea set   *Fig. 22 (above):* The Lady at the Tea Table *(detail), 1883*

Fig. 23 (opposite): The Lady at the Tea Table, *1883*

is also interesting to note the familiar French screen (fig. 24) that appeared a decade earlier in an unfinished painting of a sitting room, probably Mary Cassatt's.

In 1887, a year after the eighth and last Impressionist exhibition took place, the Cassatt family moved to a larger apartment on rue de Marignan, near the Avenue des Champs-Elysées, a home which the artist maintained until her death in 1926. There was room for a studio, and here she worked on a rigorous schedule, unless interrupted by family illness or extended visits from her American relatives. Friends and members of the family described the apartment in terms ranging from "comfortable" to "stuffy and old-fashioned." The furniture was a mixture of Louis XV, Louis XVI, Empire, and second Empire, surrounded by family accessories and paintings by her Impressionist colleagues. The use of particular pieces of furniture in her work reflects her preferences in decor and also shows her dependence on these pieces for design and structure. Although Cassatt usually avoided painting still lifes, she often allowed the round shapes of cups and saucers, silver trays, small pitchers, and numerous tables to play dominant roles in her paintings, echoing their figural contours, while the mirrors and chairs established strong diagonals or acted as framing devices.

Fig. 24: Interior with a French Screen, *c. 1881*

Fig. 25: The Tea, *1889–1890*

Fig. 26: The Visit, *1890–1891*

new
directions

With the end of the Impressionist group exhibitions, Cassatt found herself entering into new arrangements to guarantee the annual exhibition of her work. Along with other colleagues, she established a relationship with Paul Durand-Ruel, a respected art dealer and friend of the Impressionists. He was successful enough to be able to show work in Paris and New York, and he was decidedly interested in Cassatt, both as an artist and as a well-connected American abroad.

The 1890s were significant for Cassatt. An earlier, extended visit by her older brother's family had introduced her to the subject of mother and children, a motif she went on to develop in all media. The death of her sister in 1882, followed by the death of her father in late 1891, were striking blows to someone whose familial relationships were profoundly important to both her personal and her artistic life. Her relatives were remarkable, willing, and handsome models for many of her finest works.

In the spring of 1890 a visit to the great exhibition of Japanese art held at the École des Beaux Arts stimulated the artist and, once again, the course of her artistic endeavors changed. The profusion of color woodcuts and illustrated books and albums inspired Cassatt to embark on an innovative project. For an exhibition at Durand-Ruel in the spring of 1891, she produced a set of ten color prints in "imitation of the Japanese print," a subject she had studied for years. By this time, Cassatt had surrounded herself with blue and white china, numerous woodcuts, many by Utamaro (fig. 27), and several Japanese screens, indicating her affection for excellent design and superb colors. An early-eighteenth-century, six-panel screen of the four seasons (fig. 28), attributed to Ogata Kenzan (1663–1743), originally belonged to Mary Cassatt and was acquired by a young artist friend from Philadelphia, Henry McCarter, who studied in Paris.

Fig. 27: Kitagawa Utamaro (1753–1806), Two Courtesans and a Child

As a group, the ten color prints represent a major contribution to the field of printmaking in terms of unique and inventive technical processes. In light of her depictions of women and children in domestic settings, these prints are highly original. *The Letter* (fig. 30), for example, depicts an object that appears only once in her oeuvre and suggests the extensive correspondence that Cassatt herself participated in with family and friends, both at home and abroad. The artist incorporated in this print a desk from her Paris apartment (fig. 29), the writing surface of which was covered with a brilliant blue felt. This frequently used piece of furniture dictated the subject matter of the print as well as the strong blue of the flowered dress, the writing surface, and, in some impressions, even the patterned wallpaper.

The interior settings, the stylish contemporary women, and the ornaments she included in these distinctive prints represent Cassatt's adaptation and transformation of the *japonisme* vocabulary. Within the series, there is an unfolding of the same models and a repetition of daily routines—morning errands, afternoon

Fig. 28: Eighteenth-century six-panel Japanese screen attributed to Ogata Kenzan

visits, evening socializing, and bedtime rituals—all of which follow the diurnal cycles observed in surveys of Japanese woodcuts.

The fashion historian Louis Octave Uzanne described this world as one in which women of the "upper-class bourgeoisie"—Mary Cassatt's milieu—led a more private life centered around their children; they shopped at the new department stores, acquired a stunning but modest wardrobe, visited friends, and maintained a refined but subdued social life.[10]

Young Woman Trying on a Dress (fig. 31), *Nude Child*, and *Study (*familiarly known as *The Coiffure)* brilliantly illustrate the fashionable and domestic existence of Cassatt's models. The dress that is being fitted in the print, for example,

Fig. 29: Fall-front secretary used in Cassatt's Paris apartment

Fig. 30: **The Letter,** *1890–1891*

Fig. 31: Young Woman Trying on a Dress, *1890–1891*

Fig. 32: Revery, *1891–1892*

Fig. 34: Nude Child, *1890–1891*

Fig. 33 (opposite): Mother and Child, *1889*

is worn by the same model holding a zinnia in *Revery*, 1891–1892 (fig. 32), confirming Cassatt's preference for her subjects to be dressed in up-to-date fashions. When each copper plate for the color prints was inked, the combination of stripes, lines, and multiple patterns produced handsome results and many variations in color. *Nude Child* (fig. 34; familiarly known as *Maternal Caress*) recalls paintings such as *Mother and Child*, 1889 (fig. 33), with similar poses of the figures as well as distinctive coloration, sensitive placement of the hands, and an emphasis on emotional unity. The recognizable flowered dress appears in Cassatt's earlier portraits, both printed and painted. In the coiffure study (fig. 37), there is a connection to the painting of a young girl arranging her hair. The latter, called *Study* when first exhibited in 1886 (fig. 36) and given to Degas in exchange for a pastel, depicts a similar red-haired model in a room with the familiar reddish, floral wallpaper. Although it is tempting to suggest that the same decorated room is shown in both works, Cassatt changed apartments in 1887; the print could be a memoir of the painting that she had given to Degas after the eighth and last Impressionist exhibition.[11]

All of Cassatt's 1891 color series are interior settings with the exception of one print, *Interior of a Tramway Passing by a Bridge* (fig. 35). Although it is essentially an outdoor composition, it is, nevertheless, enclosed in a compact setting evocative of an inside living space. It maintains the sequence of daily practices and supplements Cassatt's other color prints of domestic scenes.

Fig. 35: Interior of a Tramway Passing by a Bridge, *1890–1891*

Fig. 36: Study, *c. 1886*

Fig. 37: Study, *1890–1891*

A CONSTANT SOURCE:

woman

One of the artist's great masterpieces is *The Child's Bath*, 1893 (fig. 38), a painting that combines the composition and subject matter of Japanese prints with the artist's Impressionist sensibility and her remarkable gift for depicting the private world of a mother and her child. The various patterns, including the floral wallpaper and the painted chest, the richly colored rug, the distinctive striped dress, and the oriental perspective are part of the Japanese precepts and also reflect Cassatt's great attachment to her personal accessories. Just as Degas judiciously placed pitchers or sprinkling cans in many of his paintings, Cassatt, too, did not hesitate to give prominence to her own everyday ceramic pieces; see, for example, the handsome basin and pitcher with their fine gold edges.

Following the completion of *The Child's Bath*, Cassatt was invited by an American committee to produce a mural for the Woman's Building of the Chicago World's Columbian Exposition in 1893. Her subject was "Modern Woman," and although it was well received by her Chicago friends and mentioned by critics, she was actually more pleased that Durand-Ruel was giving her a first retrospective exhibition in Paris. The presentation at the important gallery comprised paintings, pastels, black-and-white prints with a series of twelve drypoints, and her ten color prints. There were ninety-eight works in the exhibition—three were lent by Edgar Degas, including the study of the young girl arranging her hair—and a small catalog included an introduction by the symbolist critic, André Mellerio.

The success of the exhibition established Cassatt financially so that she could purchase a permanent country home in the Oise valley (north of Paris). With the enthusiastic response of the French audience, she was encouraged to consider a major show in New York, which came about at Durand-Ruel's New York galleries in 1895; she

and child

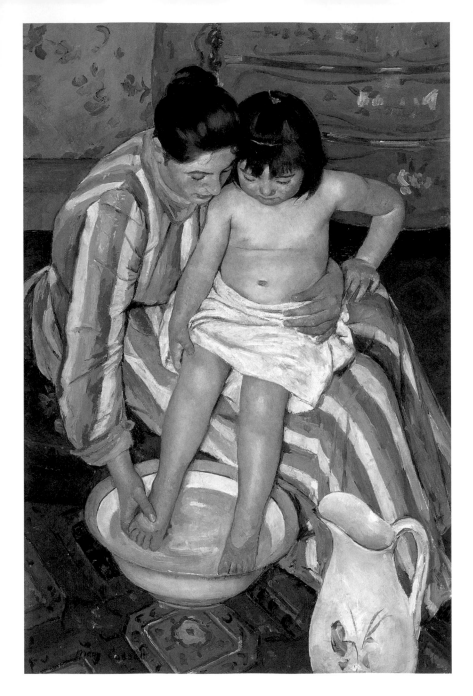

was finally able to enjoy an official presentation to the American public. She received much praise, and new buyers of her work were plentiful.

In late 1895, after Cassatt completed renovations on her seventeenth-century manor house and moved in, her mother died. Although her nursing responsibilities had come to an end, she was deeply affected by this loss, and her work, for a time, reflected this depression. In a letter to a Boston friend, Miss Rose Lamb, written in January 1898 during her first trip to America in twenty-five years, she remarked: "I lost my mother two years ago in October and was so bereft and so tired of life that I thought I could not live; now I know I must and I am here to see quite a new world and renew old ties."[12]

Cassatt's younger brother, Gardner, recognized his sister's grief and family needs and came with his wife and children to Europe for a two-year visit. During the first winter, they stayed with the artist, at which time she probably made the portrait *Ellen Mary in a White Coat*, about 1896 (fig. 41). The formal setting and elaborate costume recall the noble portraits of children by the Spanish artist Velázquez. Here the gold upholstered chair becomes a significant framing device and can be seen in many other later works by the artist. The chair's brown strips echo the sinuous fur trim of the coat and hat; family members recall that it was considered a very special and festive costume to be worn only on certain occasions. Once again, Cassatt elaborated upon the whites of the hat and coat and added more color—touches of blue-gray and yellow. By this time, the brushstrokes are lengthy and her painting surfaces are no longer built up with short touches of color.

Fig. 38: The Child's Bath, *1893*

Fig. 39: The Mirror, *c. 1905*

Fig. 40: Breakfast in Bed, *1897*

It is acknowledged that the maternal theme became the most significant subject matter of Cassatt's mature style, and in 1897 she completed one of her strongest renditions of a mother and child. In *Breakfast in Bed* (fig. 40), Cassatt depicts an attractive waking mother who enjoys an intimate moment with her child. The bedding, nightclothes, serving plate, cup, and saucer are expertly painted in various shades of white that recall the creative hand of the artist when she made the portrait of her mother in 1878. The impressionist style of short brushstrokes is also evident in the high color of the figures. Of great importance to the composition are the green headboard and corner table, part of a set of painted furniture that belonged to the artist. Cassatt used these beds, chairs, and tables as compositional supports and color notes for many of her most engaging late paintings, pastels, and prints.

About 1905, Cassatt produced another mother and child painting entitled *The Mirror* (fig. 39). Although more coarsely painted, with broad strokes, the artist remained true to her subject matter and was still attached to many of her favorite decorative accessories. The small, ornate hand mirror, a prized object that still exists, appears in other works; and the extended reflection in the large green-framed mirror, which matches the chair, recalls the reflections of images that she used in her great theater paintings of the 1870s. The opposition of round and straight forms is secure in this painting yet the relationship of the mother and child and the definition of the paint strokes is less fixed; nevertheless, the flowing gown, distinctive sunflower decoration, and luscious colors make this another successful work in Cassatt's oeuvre.

Fig. 41: Ellen Mary in a White Coat, *c. 1896*

In the early decades of the twentieth century, Cassatt had resolved her style, subject matter, and techniques. The mother and child theme was a constant subject and provided an armature for her late compositions. She painted frequently but often turned to pastels, a technique she had mastered and found more comfortable to use in her later years. Her possessions and home and studio environments still provided the settings for her masterworks, and, until her eyesight began to fail, she continued to arrange compositions, drawing upon her favorite subjects and models, and incorporating her prized possessions.

The final years

In 1906 her older brother Aleck died unexpectedly, and in 1911 a long trip to Egypt with her younger brother Gardner and his family (fig. 42) ended when he became seriously ill; he died upon his return to Paris. The loss of the last member of her immediate family was devastating to Cassatt, who could no longer rely upon the distinct personalities of her family to inspire her work. By 1915 Cassatt was frustrated in her attempts to continue painting and making prints, and, sadly, after completing some late pastels, she was obliged to abandon her artistic efforts. Mrs. J. Montgomery Sears of Boston, a good friend of the artist who frequently visited her in Paris, acquired a box of Cassatt's pastels; they still exist today.

Cassatt endured World War I, and her home eventually became a mecca for young artists, particularly those from America who sought her out as an authority on a period of art history that revolutionized her world and theirs. She remained opinionated and willful but forever willing to share.

On June 14, 1926, Mary Cassatt died at her country home and was buried nearby in Mesnil-Théribus. All her worldly possessions and personal belongings were left to the children of her brother Gardner. From her earliest years of productivity into the 1890s, when she was at the height of her career, Cassatt constantly strengthened her originality of vision and technical inventiveness. Most important, she conceived of Impressionism within the framework of the world she knew best. Mary Cassatt may be identified with her depictions of the maternal theme, but many of her most distinguished works are those which give an insight into her home and her possessions: porcelains, Persian vases, old silver, Japanese woodcuts, and other objets d'art that amateurs like herself and her parents accumulated. This major woman artist of the last decades of the nineteenth century was a compelling figure in the male-dominated art scene of Impressionism. It is especially poignant that much of her success depended on a circumscribed, elegant environment created by her family, close friends, and, as Gustave Geffroy noted in 1893, her "very elegant taste for things . . . as well as a unique grace and will."[13]

Fig. 42: Photograph of Mary Cassatt and Gardner Cassatt's family at the Pyramids, 1910

WORKS BY MARY STEVENSON CASSATT, 1844–1926

(Note: The titles and dates below are those presently assigned by the respective insitutions owning each Cassatt work and may differ from those cited by the author, who employed the original titles used from the first public exhibition of each work.)

Afternoon Tea Party, c. 1891. Color drypoint and aquatint on laid paper. $16^{3}/_{4}$ x $12^{1}/_{4}$ in. (425 x 311 cm). National Gallery of Art. Chester Dale Collection. Photograph © Board of Trustees, National Gallery of Art, Washington, D.C.

At the Opera, 1879. Oil on canvas. $31^{1}/_{2}$ x $25^{1}/_{2}$ in. (80 x 64.8 cm). Courtesy Museum of Fine Arts, Boston. Charles Henry Hayden Fund, 1910.

Breakfast in Bed, 1897. Oil on canvas. 23 x 29 in. (58.4 x 73.6 cm). The Huntington Library, Art Collections, and Botanical Gardens, San Marino, California. Gift of the Virginia Steele Scott Foundation.

The Child's Bath, 1891–1892. Oil on canvas. $39^{1}/_{2}$ x 26 in. (100.3 x 66 cm). The Art Institute of Chicago. The Robert A. Waller Fund. Photograph © The Art Institute of Chicago. All Rights Reserved.

The Coiffure, c. 1891. Drypoint and softground etching in color. The National Gallery of Art. Rosenwald Collection. Photograph © 1998 Board of Trustees, National Gallery of Art, Washington, D.C.

The Cup of Tea, 1879. Oil on canvas. $36^{3}/_{8}$ x $25^{3}/_{4}$ in. (92.4 x 65.4 cm). The Metropolitan Museum of Art, New York. From the collection of James Stillman, gift of Dr. Ernest G. Stillman, 1922 (22.16.17). © 1983 The Metropolitan Museum of Art.

Ellen Mary in a White Coat, c. 1896. Oil on canvas. 32 x $23^{3}/_{4}$ in. (81.3 x 60.3 cm). Courtesy Museum of Fine Arts, Boston.

The Fitting, 1891. Color drypoint and aquatint. $14^{3}/_{4}$ x $10^{1}/_{8}$ in. (platemark); $18^{7}/_{8}$ x $12^{1}/_{8}$ in. (sheet). Courtesy Museum of Fine Arts, Boston. Gift of William Emerson and Charles Henry Hayden Fund, 1941.

Girl Arranging Her Hair, c. 1886. Oil on canvas. $29^{5}/_{8}$ x $24^{3}/_{8}$ in. (75.2 x 62.5 cm). National Gallery of Art. The Chester Dale Collection. Photograph © Board of Trustees, National Gallery of Art, Washington, D.C.

Interior with a French Screen, c. 1881. Oil on canvas. 17 x $22^{1}/_{2}$ in. (43 x 57 cm). By permission of owner.

In the Omnibus, 1891. Drypoint, softground etching, and aquatint. Courtesy Museum of Fine Arts, Boston. Gift of William Emerson and Charles Henry Hayden Fund, 1941.

In the Opera Box, 1879–1880. Etching. Courtesy Museum of Fine Arts, Boston.

The Lady at the Tea Table, 1883. Oil on canvas. 29 x 24 in. (73.4 x 61 cm). The Metropolitan Museum of Art, New York. Gift of the artist (23.101). © 1994 The Metropolitan Museum of Art.

The Letter, 1890–1891. Drypoint and aquatint printed in color. 43.7 x 29.7 cm. The Art Institute of Chicago. Martin A. Ryerson Collection, 1932.1282. Photograph © The Art Institute of Chicago. All Rights Reserved.

Little Girl in a Blue Armchair, 1878. Oil on canvas. $35\frac{1}{4}$ x $51\frac{1}{8}$ in. (89.5 x 129.8 cm). National Gallery of Art. Collection of Mr. And Mrs. Paul Mellon. Photograph © The Board of Trustees, National Gallery of Art, Washington, D.C.

Lydia at Afternoon Tea, c. 1880. Drypoint and aquatint. $5\frac{1}{2}$ x $7\frac{7}{8}$ in. Private Collection. Courtesy Museum of Fine Arts, Boston.

Lydia at a Tapestry Frame, c. 1881. Oil on canvas. $25\frac{5}{8}$ x $36\frac{3}{8}$ in. (65 x 92.4 cm). Courtesy Flint Institute of Arts. Gift of the Whiting Foundation.

Lydia Crocheting in the Garden at Marly, 1880. Oil on canvas. 26 x 37 in. (66 x 94 cm). The Metropolitan Museum of Art, New York. Gift of Mrs. Gardner Cassatt, 1965 (65.184). © 1993 The Metropolitan Museum of Art.

Maternal Caress, c. 1891. Drypoint and softground etching. $16\frac{13}{16}$ x $12\frac{5}{16}$ in. (42.7 x 31.2 cm). National Gallery of Art. The Rosenwald Collection. Photograph © Board of Trustees, National Gallery of Art, Washington, D.C.

Mother and Child, c. 1890. Oil on canvas. $35\frac{3}{8}$ x $25\frac{3}{8}$ in. (89.8 x 64.4 cm). Witchita Art Museum. The Roland P. Murdock Collection.

Mother and Child (Mother Wearing a Sunflower on Her Dress), c. 1905. Oil on canvas. $36\frac{1}{4}$ x 29 in. (92.1 x 73.7 cm). National Gallery of Art. The Chester Dale Collection. Photograph © Board of Trustees, National Gallery of Art, Washington, D.C.

Portrait of a Young Woman in Black, 1883. Oil on canvas. $31\frac{13}{16}$ x $25\frac{1}{2}$ in. (80.8 x 64.8 cm). The Peabody Institute of the City of Baltimore, on extended loan to The Baltimore Museum of Art.

Reading Le Figaro, 1877–1878. Oil on canvas. $39\frac{3}{4}$ x 32 in. (101 x 81.2 cm). Private collection, Washington, D.C.

The Tea, 1880. Oil on canvas. $25\frac{1}{2}$ x $36\frac{1}{4}$ in. (64.8 x 92.7 cm). Courtesy Museum of Fine Arts, Boston. The M. Theresa B. Hopkins Fund.

The Tea, 1889–1890. Drypoint. 7 x $6\frac{1}{8}$ in. Private collection. Courtesy Museum of Fine Arts, Boston.

The Visit, c. 1881. Softground, aquatint, drypoint and etching. $15\frac{5}{8}$ x $12\frac{1}{8}$ in. © Sterling and Francine Clark Art Institute, Williamstown, Massachusetts.

Woman with a Pearl Necklace in a Loge, 1879. Oil on canvas. $31\frac{5}{8}$ x 23 in. Philadelphia Museum of Art. Bequest of Charlotte Dorrance Wright.

Woman with a Red Zinnia, 1891. Oil on canvas. 20 x $23\frac{3}{4}$ in. (73.6 x 60.3 cm). National Gallery of Art. The Chester Dale Collection. Photograph © Board of Trustees, National Gallery of Art, Washington, D.C.

Woman Reading (Portrait of Lydia Cassatt, the Artist's Sister), 1878–1979. Oil on canvas. 32 x $23\frac{1}{2}$ in. (81.2 x 59.6 cm). Joslyn Art Museum, Omaha, Nebraska.

TURED WORKS

OTHER FEATURED WORKS

Blue and white Chinese export tea service, c. 1780–1800. Porcelain, fluted, with gilt overpainting. Teapot: height $4\frac{1}{2}$ in. (11.4 cm).

Edgar Degas, 1834–1917. *Mary Cassatt at the Louvre: The Etruscan Gallery*, 1879–1880. Softground etching, drypoint, aquatint, and etching. 26.9 x 23.3 cm. Courtesy Museum of Fine Arts, Boston. Katherine E. Bullard Fund in memory of Francis Bullard and proceeds from the sale of duplicate prints.

Edgar Degas, 1834–1917. *Mary Cassatt at the Louvre: The Paintings Gallery*, 1879–1880. Etching, drypoint, and aquatint. 30.3 x 12.7 cm. Courtesy of Museum of Fine Arts, Boston. Katherine E. Bullard Fund in memory of Francis Bullard and proceeds from the sale of duplicate prints.

Edgar Degas, 1834–1917. *Fan Mount: Ballet Girls*, 1879. Watercolor, silver and gold on silk. $7\frac{1}{2}$ x $22\frac{3}{4}$ in. (19.1 x 57.8 cm). The Metropolitan Museum of Art, H. O. Havemeyer Collection, Bequest of Mrs. H. O. Havemeyer, 1929 (20.100.555). © 1987 The Metropolitan Museum of Art.

Eighteenth-century Japanese screen attributed to Ogata Kenzan (1663–1743). Six-panel folding screen with pigments over gold leaf. $16\frac{1}{2}$ x 146 in. (176 x 371 cm). Philadelphia Museum of Art. Goerge W. B. Taylor Fund.

Edouard Manet, 1832–1883. *Le Repos: Portrait of Berthe Morisot*, c. 1870. Oil on canvas. $59\frac{1}{8}$ x $47\frac{7}{8}$ in. Museum of Art, Rhode Island School of Design. Bequest of the Estate of Mrs. Edith Stuyvesant Vanderbilt Gerry.

Fall-front secretary. France, c. 1790. Mahogany and mahogany veneers on oak. Height 62 in. (157.5 cm). Museum of Fine Arts, Boston. Anonymous gift in honor of Margaret K. Cassatt and Gardner Cassatt, 1997.51.

Photograph of Mary Cassatt with the Gardner family at the Pyramids, 1910. Approximately 7 x 9 in. Private collection. Courtesy Museum of Fine Arts, Boston.

Theodate Pope. Photograph of Mary Cassatt at Beaufresne, 1903. Photograph courtesy of the Hill-Stead Museum, Farmington, Connecticut.

Silver tea set. Maker: Philip Garrett, active 1801–1835. Teapot: height $7\frac{1}{2}$ in. (19.3 cm). Museum of Fine Arts, Boston. Anonymous gift in honor of Eugenia Cassatt Madeira, 1982.

Tureen, dinner plate, and dessert plate: *Fleurs et rubans*. France, 1879–1880. Designed by Félix Braquemond (1833–1914). Made in Creil Montereau factory for Haviland & Co. Faience. Tureen: 10 in. (25.4 cm). Private collection.

Kitagawa Utamaro (1753–1806). *Two Courtesans and a Child*. Color woodcut. $14\frac{1}{2}$ x $10\frac{1}{2}$ in. (37 x 25.7 cm). Courtesy Museum of Fine Arts, Boston.

NOTES

1 Cited in *Cassatt: A Retrospective*, edited by Nancy Mowll Mathews (Southport, Conn: Hugh Lauter Levin Associates, Inc.), 1996, p. 132. The full text in French is found in *Documentation, Volume I: Reviews*, edited by Ruth Berson, (San Francisco: Fine Arts Museums of San Francisco, 1996), p. 350. (*Documentation* is a comprehensive, two-volume catalog of all the Impressionist exhibitions, expanding upon the original exhibition catalog titled *The New Painting: Impressionism 1874–1886*, edited by Charles S. Moffett, et al., 1986.)

2 Cited in *The New Painting*, p. 276. For full text in Italian, see *Documentation, Volume I*, p. 219.

3 *The New Painting*, p. 277. See also *Documentation, Volume I*, p. 219.

4 *The New Painting*, p. 277. See also *Documentation, Volume I*, p. 243 (under F. -C. de Syène).

5 *The New Painting*, p. 321. See also *Documentation, Volume I*, p. 306 (written 24 April, 1880).

6 *The New Painting*, p. 302. See also *Documentation, Volume I*, p. 297.

7 Cited in *Cassatt: A Retrospective*, p. 132. See also *Documentation, Volume I*, p. 350.

8 Cited in *Cassatt: A Retrospective*, p. 98 (from *May Alcott: A Memoir*, 1928).

9 Cited in *Cassatt: A Retrospective*, p. 135.

10 See Valerie Steele, *Paris Fashion* (New York: Oxford University Press, 1988), p. 188, for her reference to Louis Octave Uzanne, *La Femme à Paris*, (Paris, 1894).

11 Cited by Mathews in Nancy Mowll Mathews and Barbara Stern Shapiro, *Mary Cassatt: The Color Prints*, exhibition catalog (New York: Harry N. Abrams, 1989), p. 151.

12 Cited in Barbara Stern Shapiro, *Mary Cassatt at Home*, exhibition catalog (Boston: Museum of Fine Arts, 1978), p. 9.

13 Cited in *Cassatt: A Retrospective*, p. 99.